At Issue

Should Parents Be Allowed to Choose the Sex of Their Children?

D1373888

Other Books in the At Issue Series:

Alcohol Abuse

Alternatives to Prisons

Are Books Becoming Extinct?

Are Mass Extinctions Inevitable?

Biodiesel

Cancer

Cyberpredators

Distracted Driving

Do Students Have Too Much Homework?

Food Insecurity

Gay Marriage

Genetically Engineered Food

Guns and Crime

Health Care Legislation

Organ Transplants

Policing the Internet

Should Tasers Be Legal?

Standardized Testing

Will the World Run Out of Fresh Water?

At Issue

Should Parents Be Allowed to Choose the Sex of Their Children?

Tamara Thompson, Book Editor

GREENHAVEN PRESS
A part of Gale, Cengage Learning

GALE
CENGAGE Learning·

Detroit • New York • San Francisco • New Haven, Conn • Waterville, Maine • London

Elizabeth Des Chenes, *Managing Editor*

© 2012 Greenhaven Press, a part of Gale, Cengage Learning.

Gale and Greenhaven Press are registered trademarks used herein under license.

For more information, contact:
Greenhaven Press
27500 Drake Rd.
Farmington Hills, MI 48331-3535
Or you can visit our Internet site at gale.cengage.com

For product information and technology assistance, contact us at

Gale Customer Support, 1-800-877-4253
For permission to use material from this text or product, submit all requests online at www.cengage.com/permissions.

Further permissions questions can be e-mailed to permissionrequest@cengage.com.

Articles in Greenhaven Press anthologies are often edited for length to meet page require- ments. In addition, original titles of these works are changed to clearly present the main thesis and to explicitly indicate the author's opinion. Every effort is made to ensure that Greenhaven Press accurately reflects the original intent of the authors. Every effort has been made to trace the owners of copyrighted material.

Cover image copyright © Images.com/Corbis.

LIBRARY OF CONGRESS CATALOGING-IN-PUBLICATION DATA

Should parents be allowed to choose the sex of their children? / Tamara Thomp- son, book editor.
        p. cm. -- (At issue)
    Includes bibliographical references and index.
    ISBN 978-0-7377-5594-7 (hardcover) -- ISBN 978-0-7377-5595-4 (pbk.)
    1. Sex preselection--Moral and ethical aspects. 2. Sex preselection--Social as- pects. 3. Sex of children, Parental preferences for. I. Thompson, Tamara.
    QP279.S57 2011
    362.196'8583--dc23
                                                          2011047010

Printed in the United States of America
  2 3 4 5 6   16 15 14 13 12
FD226

Contents

Introduction   7

1. Sex Selection Is Not Ethical   11
   Sujatha Jesudason

2. Sex Selection Is Ethical   19
   Austin Cline

3. Sex Selection Should Be Regulated   24
   Hattie Kauffman

4. Sex Selection Can Lead to
   Gender Discrimination   28
   Generations Ahead

5. Sex Selection Will Not Lead to
   Gender Discrimination   40
   Edgar Dahl

6. Women Should Have the Right to Choose
   the Sex of Their Children   48
   Christine Hicks

7. Sex Selection Can Lead to
   Trait-Based Eugenics   54
   Gautam Naik

8. Sex Selection Leads to Gendercide
   in China and India   61
   The Economist

9. Sex-Selective Abortion Should Be Banned   66
   Trent Franks

10. Banning Sex-Selective Abortion Would
    Imperil Reproductive Freedom   71
    Generations Ahead

Organizations to Contact   75

Bibliography   81

Index   87

Introduction

One hundred sixty million is roughly the number of women and girls who are alive in the United States today; it's also roughly the number of females who are *not* alive in Asia because prenatal ultrasounds and sex-selective abortions have enabled women to avoid bearing girls in favor of having sons. Although the phenomenon isn't limited to Asia—skewed birth ratios appear in the Balkans and Caucasus regions as well—China (with 121 boys per 100 girls), India (112 to 100), and Vietnam (111 to 100) show the most lopsided numbers. The normal human birth ratio is 105 boys to 100 girls, a ratio that promotes population stability and social harmony, according to many social scientists. Any significant deviation is thought to result in negative consequences for a society.

While many observers decry the birth ratio phenomenon as "gendercide" against women and argue that blatant gender discrimination and cultural preferences for sons lie at the heart of the disparity, other less obvious factors may contribute even more to the crisis.

In her 2011 book *Unnatural Selection: Choosing Boys Over Girls, and the Consequences of a World Full of Men*, journalist Mara Hvistendahl breaks new ground by arguing that the problem is primarily rooted in rising global wealth and the spread of Western attitudes and technology, rather than cultural gender bias against females.

Hvistendahl maintains that "blaming backward cultural traditions is simpler than the alternative of taking a hard look at how a particular phenomenon—including the technology that makes that phenomenon possible—came to exist."

As Hvistendahl points out, economic progress means that more girls go to school and have access to better job opportunities when they grow up. As women become more socially and economically empowered, they also come to value having smaller families; their countries similarly value a declining birth rate as a sign of modernization. When urban, educated women do have children, they are more likely to be able to afford access to modern health care—including ultrasounds that can determine the sex of a fetus and abortions to terminate unwanted pregnancies.

"Because development is accompanied by plummeting birth rates," Hvistendahl writes, "it raises the stakes for each birth, increasing the chances parents will abort a female fetus. This triangle of concurrent trends—development, falling fertility, and sex selection—is alarming because it means sex selection won't simply disappear."

As reproductive technology becomes cheaper and more widely available, access to sex-selective technologies—as well as the attitudes about utilizing them—are passed down the socioeconomic ladder from the early-adopter rich to the emerging global middle class, and then ultimately to the masses.

"By the time the technology reaches the lower classes," notes Hvistendahl, "the elite is often ready to move on to the next big thing."

Indeed, as the developing world grapples with the stunning consequences of readily available ultrasounds and abortions, in the United States the focus is on a new generation of reproductive technologies, such as preimplantation genetic diagnosis (PGD), a procedure that can identify the sex of a fertilized embryo before it is implanted in the womb during in vitro fertilization (IVF). Developed to screen embryos for life threatening conditions, PGD is now also commonly used to determine the sex of embryos for "family balancing" purposes during the expensive IVF process ($12,000–$15,000 on average). Some fertility clinics offer sex-selective PGD for nonmedical reasons altogether. A 2006 survey by the Genetics and Public Policy Center at Johns Hopkins University found that of the responding American fertility clinics that perform PGD, 42 percent offer sex selection for social reasons. One in one hundred American babies is currently born through IVF, but it is unclear how many of those babies have been chosen for their sex via PGD.

Although bans on sex-selective abortion have passed or are pending in ten states (despite limited use of the practice in the United States), there is no such formal regulation of PGD. According to the website BioPolicyWiki (www.biopolicy wiki.org), while sex selection for nonmedical reasons is prohibited in thirty-six countries, reproductive technologies such as PGD are spreading unregulated throughout the developing world. PGD is already offered in Brazil, China, Cyprus, Egypt, India, Jordan, Mexico, Russia, and Thailand. As with ultrasounds and sex-selective abortion (which is widespread despite being illegal in many places), PGD will eventually trickle down to the middle class worldwide as the technology becomes cheaper and more accessible.

With the advent of a new blood test, however, concerns about the global creep of PGD and similar technologies have been overshadowed.

On August 20, 2011, *The New York Times* reported a simple new blood test that uses DNA to determine a fetus's sex. The test can accurately identify a boy or girl with 95 percent certainty as early as seven weeks into pregnancy. *The Times*'s assessment that the test—already available at drugstores and online—could "alter the landscape of American pregnancy" is no overstatement. Not only is the test earlier than an ultrasound and less invasive and safer than amniocentesis (a procedure in which a long needle is inserted into the womb to draw out amniotic fluid), but it can be done in the privacy of one's own home, and near the beginning of a pregnancy. Then, if termination is desired, that can be done discreetly, too; the prescription abortion drug RU-486 (mifepristone) can be used at home before ten weeks of gestation—before most pregnancies even show.

"I think over the long run this has the potential of changing attitudes toward pregnancy and to family," Audrey R. Chapman, a bioethicist at the University of Connecticut Health Center told *The New York Times*. "Women may be less invested in their pregnancies earlier than they are later, and the question has been raised whether women will look at their pregnancies increasingly as being conditional: 'I will keep this pregnancy only if.'"

What impact the new blood test will have—both in the United States and as it becomes available globally—remains to be seen, but if other sex-selective technologies are any indicator, it won't be insignificant. As San Francisco internist Sunita Puri told columnist Debra J. Saunders in a July 2011 *San Francisco Chronicle* article about sex selection: "The technology moves faster than the discussion, and we have no data on the short- and long-term consequences of what we're doing."

The authors in *At Issue: Should Parents Be Allowed to Choose the Sex of Their Children?* examine the various types of sex-selection techniques practiced around the world today and assess the ethics and consequences of their use, both for the present day and for future generations.

1

Sex Selection Is Not Ethical

Sujatha Jesudason

Sujatha Jesudason is the program director on gender, justice and human genetics at the Center for Genetics and Society, a non-profit organization that works to encourage responsible uses and effective societal governance of the new human genetic and reproductive technologies.

Reproductive medicine and its emerging genetic and biotechnological technologies are, first and foremost, women's issues. As such procedures as embryo sex selection, preimplantation genetic diagnosis (PGD), and genetic modification become more commonly accepted and prevalent, so too does their underlying effect of causing violence against women and against future generations of humans. As women's bodies become more and more medicalized and viewed as raw material to manipulate, it has the potential to endanger not only women's health but also basic fundamentals of human equality and human rights. "Market-driven eugenics," such as PGD, causes discrimination to be practiced against certain types of humans, for example the deaf, those with Down syndrome, or even females as a group. Selective reproductive technologies like sex selection are not ethical and they raise very troubling moral and societal questions that must be addressed before the practices become more firmly established.

I was born into a culture that embraces confusing messages about the worth and value of women. I grew up in an India where a woman such as Indira Gandhi could become a formi-

Sujatha Jesudason, "The Future of Violence Against Women: Human Rights & the New Genetics," *Center for Genetics and Society*, February 21, 2006. Used by permission of the author.

dable leader, and yet female infants were routinely killed or starved because they were deemed less valuable than boys. This contradiction played out in my family where smart and competent women who made a difference in the world continued to live with men who abused them, or attempted suicide when their husbands left them. The female role models in my life oscillated between these radical extremes: powerful agents and value-less victims. For as much as I have resisted, this confusion has been a central struggle in my life; I have worked to believe that there is a place for me in this world, that I have a right to enjoyment and happiness, that I matter, and that I have the power to make a difference.

Women's bodies and women's eggs are the raw materials of these new human biotechnologies—what forms of violence are they and will they perpetuate against women, and against future generations?

Cycles of Violence

I began working to end violence against women nearly fifteen years ago when I realized that violence is one of the key tools of women's oppression. Not only does this violence literally beat us into submission but, like female infanticide, it inscribes messages of powerlessness, worthlessness and vulnerability onto our bodies, minds and spirits. For many women, this kind of physical and emotional vulnerability begins early and carries through into adulthood, when we struggle to understand how we matter, that we have bodily and emotional integrity, and that we deserve respect and have rights.

As future science and biotechnology, in the form of stem cell research and reproductive genetic technologies, started insistently knocking at our public door, I started to think about the future forms of violence against women. Women's bodies and women's eggs are the raw materials of these new human biotechnologies—what forms of violence are they and will they perpetuate against women, and against future generations? While there have been many beneficial reproductive technological developments, we are also at a cross-roads where many of the technologies currently in use and under consideration—sex selection, pre-implantation genetic diagnosis, reproductive cloning and inheritable genetic modification—have the potential to endanger women's health, and, moreover, threaten basic notions of human equality and human rights.

Troubling Questions

If we consider the different kinds of reproductive screening technologies promoted in the U.S. today, we can see the kind of troubling questions these technologies raise for women. Women's bodies are increasingly medicalized in these processes now, and women are under increasing pressures to produce particular kinds of children, whether they be of a particular sex or ability.

We are looking at one of the new forms of violence against women.

What's equally disquieting is that some of these practices are market-driven. Sex selection processes like MicroSort, a form of pre-conception sperm sorting, are being advertised as "family balancing" and "gender diversity" innocently asking, "Do you want to choose the gender of your next baby?" Technologies such as amniocentesis and pre-implantation genetic diagnosis have long been controversial among disability rights advocates, raising concerns about the normalization of selection processes and eugenic notions of desirable and undesirable traits. As these technologies develop, there are many who advocate that they be used not only for cures, but also for enhancement. They see no problem with women's eggs and genetic material being harvested and manipulated to modify future generations for specific eye color, faster twitch muscles, increased intelligence, decreased need for sleep, narrower emotional capacity (to prevent depression), or any other futuristic notion of what a "better" human being should look like, act like or feel.

The Worth of a Woman

As the new reproductive and genetic technologies continue to develop, which messages will be programmed into women's minds, bodies and spirits as mothers? What about future generations of women in terms of their value, worth and power in the world? Will a woman's worth be determined by the "perfection" of the children she bears? Will a baby's value be determined by the amount of money a parent can spend to "buy" the screening processes and genetic modifications? Will a girl's worth be measured by how well she fits the gendered stereotypes in her parents' mind when they selected for her using MicroSort? What will be the value and worth of "designed" children, and of children whose parents could not afford to preselect the traits of their children?

As somebody who has worked for many years in domestic violence prevention, particularly in the South Asian American community, I am careful about what I label as violence. With clear memories of broken and bloody bodies, I hesitate to call every violation of a woman's dignity and integrity a form of violence. And yet I watch as international scandals break out about the buying and selling of women's eggs for research with no discussion of women's health and safety concerns or the reduction of women's lives and bodies to their biological materials. We are looking at one of the new forms of violence against women.

It is in the violence against women movement that we have developed our most organized and consistent voice in our struggle for women's respect, dignity and power in the world. We have named the violence and work to stop it. And this is the movement [that] continues to most clearly advocate and organize for women's bodily integrity and human rights, and that believes in the power, worth and well-being of women and girls.

Eugenics and Women

As I think about the perilous potentials of genetic and reproductive technologies, I am deeply concerned about what they may imply for future forms of violence against women in the genetic age. Eugenics has a long track record of targeting women; sterilization, incarceration, and rape are but a few of the ways we have been used as guinea pigs and selected out of existence. This new form of eugenics will also target women's bodies, integrity and fertility. In the past, eugenics movements—movements that have tried to "breed better human beings"—have been mostly state sponsored. While the eugenic practices of Nazi Germany most often come to mind, there were significant eugenic programs of sterilization, segregation and immigration restrictions in the early 1900s in the U.S. Now, however, we face the possibility of a market-based eugenics, where individuals in the marketplace could seek to either eliminate or promote particularly "desireable" or "undesireable" genetic characteristics through genetic screening, sex selection, gene therapies and genetic modification.

The new reproductive and genetic technologies raise all kinds of complicated and confusing questions—ethically, morally and socially.

Do we have a language and a conceptual framework to articulate what these technologies will do to women's bodies, women's rights, and the value of women? We need to understand the kind of platforms of doubt and vulnerability this kind of normalization and selection will program into our culture and in our relationships with each other. And we need

15

to start talking about the kind of violence and violation that will be done to women's bodies in the name of these technologies—the kind of eugenic violence and even genocide that might get practiced against particular groups of people, whether they be girl babies in India and China, Down's syndrome children in the U.S., or the "unperfect" children of the future. What will be our message to women and children if we start designing children? What kind of conditional love are we creating and what kind of inequality are we coding in our bodies and our selves?

Distorting Society

Beyond the violations of human rights perpetuated by these technologies, these market-driven eugenics have the potential to end the human community as we know it. Some biotech advocates envision a world of "genetic castes" with the "Gen-Rich" and "Naturals", where people who are wealthy enough to afford genetic modifications will rule over those who are not modified. These technologies hold the potential to encode existing social inequalities into genetic make-up. Race and racism will no longer be merely social problems, but will be genetically engraved into our bodies. Will it be possible to ensure human equality, democracy and human rights for genetically and biologically different human beings?

So, what can we do about this? In addition to policies that ban reproductive cloning, inheritable genetic modification, and the marketing of selection procedures, we also need to start social and public discussions of the implications of these technologies. These decisions can not be left up to scientists, biotechnology corporations and policy wonks; they need to be made by people and, in particular, women and the international community.

One route into these discussions is those old-fashioned consciousness-raising groups that characterized the beginning of the second wave of feminism. In such venues we need to talk about human rights and values in these intimate, personal decisions. Just like we did with domestic violence, sexual assault, and sexual harassment, our conversations with other women can turn private struggles into public and social problems. The new reproductive and genetic technologies raise all kinds of complicated and confusing questions—ethically, morally and socially. If we can share our doubts and confusions with each other, we can gain clarity about the broader social powers at play. We need to reflect more deeply on the values and worth we will encode in the bodies of women and in future generations.

Without regulation or oversight, these technologies will violate our fundamental human rights and the very foundation of human equality.

Human Rights Must Be Protected

How do we define what it means to be human in the genetic age? Who decides who is worthy of living? Who decides if we human beings need "enhancement" and at what price to women's bodies and lives? Without regulation or oversight, these technologies will violate our fundamental human rights and the very foundation of human equality that makes possible the functioning of any democracy. We need to ensure that the rights of women, children and all humans are respected, protected and guaranteed.

In India the ethical and political understanding of these new human biotechnologies is much clearer. I could not say it any better than the Saheli Women's Resource Centre:

"The final goal of reproductive engineering appears to be the manufacture of a human being to suit exact specifications of physical attributes, class, caste, colour and sex. Who will decide these specifications? We have already seen how sex-determination has resulted in the elimination of female fe-

tuses. The powerless in any society will get more disempow-
ered with the growth of such reproductive technologies."

Over time, many women have been the target of eugenic
practices—poor women, women of color, queer women,
women with disabilities. The new reproductive and genetic
technologies hold the potential for both great promise and
great danger for women, our bodies and our communities.
Rather than let these technologies slip down the slope of becoming the next tools of violence that violate women's bodies,
dignity and integrity, let us work together in thoughtful and
ethical ways towards ensuring the future of human rights and
human equality.

2

Sex Selection Is Ethical

Austin Cline

Austin Cline is the former regional director for the Council for Secular Humanism and has been educating people about atheism, agnosticism, and secular humanism for more than fifteen years.

Most of the criticism and fears about sex selection and its potential effects on society are unfounded and are based on the Slippery Slope Fallacy, in which a relatively small first step leads to a much larger and unintended outcome. In this case the fallacy is the supposition that allowing parents to choose the sex of their child will ultimately lead to genetically desirable "designer babies" and the shunning of those individuals who are less genetically desirable—either by their parents or by society at large. Technologies for sperm sorting and sex-selecting embryos have been around for many, many years and have been ethically used in conjunction with fertility treatments, such as in vitro fertilization (the implanting of a medically fertilized embryo in a womb). If someone legitimately opposes sex selection then they should oppose in vitro treatments as well.

Should parents be able to select the gender of their child? Would it be ethical for people with fertility problems to choose which fertilized embryos get implanted and have the rest discarded as being the "wrong" gender? According to the

American Society for Reproductive Medicine, a group which establishes ethical guidelines for fertility clinics, the answers to those questions is "Yes."

Many fertility specialists around the country were shocked to hear this announcement, released in a letter written by John Robertson, an ethicist and lawyer at the University of Texas who is currently the acting head of the organization. Some, however, will be offering the service immediately and report having received many requests for it over the years.

This position does not quite represent a decision by the ethics committee of the group, because the group was unable to meet in September [2001] because of the terrorist attacks in New York City and Washington D.C. Robertson did, however, say that he consulted with others and felt that the letter reflected the group's position. The previous position of the group, decided in 1999, was that such selection "should be discouraged."

Even back in January of 2001 the ethics committee raised serious ethical questions with such gender selection, including: "the potential for inherent gender discrimination, inappropriate control over nonessential characteristics of children, unnecessary medical burdens and costs for parents, and inappropriate and potentially unfair use of limited medical resources." After all, if physicians are using their skills for non-medical reasons, then those resources cannot be brought to other individuals with genuine need.

Additional concerns people have are possible sex ratio imbalances in the future (like we already have in China and India), "psychological harm to sex-selected offspring (i.e., by placing on them too high expectations), increased marital conflict over sex selective decisions, and reinforcement of gender bias in society as a whole."

Technology Is Not New

The technology for doing this has existed for quite some time—there is nothing really new about it. However, it has been used almost exclusively for couples with legitimate fears of having babies with certain genetic diseases. For example, male embryos might be rejected because it is so likely that they may carry hemophilia. In other cases, the embryo can be genetically tested for the disease itself, and only healthy ones will be implanted.

> *It is arguable that unless there is demonstrable and substantial harm to others, then couples should be allowed to choose the gender of their offspring.*

It should be noted that the decision does [not] simply approve of widespread gender selection—instead, it approves of situation-specific actions. The particular term used by Robertson is "gender variety," by which he means that a couple who already has a child of one gender should be allowed to ethically choose the implantation of embryos which would make sure their next child was of the opposite gender.

Aside from the fact that parents have traditionally been given great discretion over their reproductive choices, the ability to aid the desires of couples who have strong preferences about the gender of their offspring is perhaps the strongest reason for allowing such work. Thus, it is arguable that unless there is demonstrable and substantial harm to others, then couples should be allowed to choose the gender of their offspring.

Robertson has also emphasized that the couple needs to be fully informed of all the risks of the procedure and that they should receive counseling regarding unrealistic expectations about the behavior of children of the sought-after gender. It would, after all, be a disservice to the child if the parents were disappointed in him or her because the child failed to live up to particular gender stereotypes.

It is no surprise that not everyone approves of this new position. Dr. James Grifo, president-elect of the Society for

Assisted Reproductive Technology, has condemned sex selection as being nothing more than sex discrimination—and, hence, as unethical. He also worries that widespread publicity and marketing of this service could ultimately lead to people rejecting the technology of "test-tube" babies and, hence, prevent doctors from helping people with genuine medical needs.

He also worries about where we, as a society, are headed once parents start choosing particular embryos based upon particular, desired traits and then discarding all of those which do not "measure up." Specifically, how will we treat those who grow up with "undesirable" traits, for example the less intelligent or the less beautiful?

If someone is really bothered by 'potential babies' being thrown away, then they should object to these fertility treatments completely.

Sperm Sorting vs. Checking Embryos

Another ethical question arises because there is already a method of gender selection which has received approval and which few object to: sperm sorting. It is possible to sort sperm into two groups, those which will produce male babies and those which will produce female babies. This technique is not, however, as reliable as checking the resulting embryo.

So, some think that if the basic concept of gender selection is ethical, then it would be *unethical* to only offer an inferior method of doing it. Others, however, see a vital ethical difference between the two methods, noting that sperm sorting does not result in discarding "potential babies."

This seems like a rather disingenuous objection, at least coming from anyone involved in the creation of embryos for fertility treatments. Why? Because they always create more than is needed, which necessarily results in some which may simply be discarded because they are superfluous. If someone really is bothered by "potential babies" being thrown away, then they should object to these fertility treatments completely.

When reading the statements of these "dueling ethicists," it is also worth wondering just what *makes* a person an "ethicist." How on earth do you become a "professional" in a field like ethics? Certainly a person can be better informed about the *facts* in a particular area, like medicine, and thus be in a better position to make informed ethical decisions in that area.

Despite some people's concerns, there is no reason to think that because we accept gender selection, society will inevitably end up creating 'designer babies' and discriminate against any child that isn't perfect.

What Is an Ethicist?

But, if we are in possession of the same information, is there any good reason to defer to an ethicist as some sort of expert or authority? Do they really qualify as someone to whom we should defer, and accept what they say as being ethical?

Despite some people's concerns, there is no reason to think that because we accept gender selection, society will inevitably end up creating "designer babies" and discriminate against any child that isn't perfect. This sort of thinking is an example of the Slippery Slope Fallacy. But if we don't go down that path, the main reason will be because we create clear ethical guidelines for exactly why gender selection is acceptable, but other sorts of selection or manipulation is not acceptable.

If, however, we are only doing it because we *can* and because there is a consumer *demand*, then the path of "designer babies" remains very much open to us, and there is every reason to think that society will take it. Clearly, then, it is incumbent upon us to create those ethical guidelines and be certain about what we are doing and why.

3

Sex Selection Should Be Regulated

Hattie Kauffman

Hattie Kauffman is an Emmy award-winning correspondent for The Early Show of CBS News, a nationally broadcast morning news program whose content is also published online at www.cbsnews.com.

The Fertility Institute in Los Angeles, California, is a cutting-edge fertility clinic that offers preimplantation genetic diagnosis, a procedure that can screen embryos for disease; it also plans to offer prospective parents the opportunity to select their future child's sex, eye color, hair color, complexion and other features using the same technology. The clinic's founder believes that such cosmetic medicine is simply another consumer choice that he can offer to his patients. Bioethicists, however, are troubled by the implications of where such technology is headed. They call for industry oversight and regulation to be put in place now so that there are clear guidelines that determine what kinds of reproductive technologies can be used and defining how they may be applied in regard to trait-based selection.

For years, reproductive specialists have been helping people become parents, even enabling them to choose the sex of their baby. One fertility doctor is taking things a step further, offering what some are calling "designer babies," as *Early Show* national correspondent Hattie Kauffman reports.

If you could design your baby's features, would you? According to L.A.'s [Los Angeles, California's] Fertility Institute,

Hattie Kauffman, "'Designer Babies' Ethical?" cbsnews.com, March 3, 2009. Used by permission.

prospective parents can select eye color, hair color and more. The technology is called pre-implantation genetic diagnosis or PGD. It was created to screen for disease, then used for gender selection. Now this clinic plans to allow parents to select physical traits.

"I would predict that by next year [2012], we will have determined sex with 100 percent certainty on a baby, and we will have determined eye color with about an 80 percent accuracy rate," said fertility specialist Dr. Jeff Steinberg, director of Fertility Institute. Dr. Jeffrey Steinberg is a pioneer in in-vitro fertilization. "I think it's very important that we not bury our head in the sand and pretend these advances are not happening," Dr. Steinberg said.

A recent U.S. survey suggests most people support the notion of building a better baby when it comes to eliminating serious diseases.

Building a Better Baby

Kirsten and Matt Landon used his clinic to select the sex of their daughter. Choosing other genetic traits intrigues them. "I would have considered trait selection as an option, but not necessarily have gone with it," Matt Landon said.

A recent U.S. survey suggests most people support the notion of building a better baby when it comes to eliminating serious diseases. But Dr. Steinberg says using technology for cosmetic reasons shouldn't scare people away.

"Of course, once I've got this science, am I not to provide this to my patients? I'm a physician. I want to provide everything science gives me to my patients," Dr. Steinberg said.

"But is that a good thing?" *Early Show* co-anchor Maggie Rodriguez asked Dr. Arthur Caplan, Ph.D, director of the Center for Bioethics at the University of Pennsylvania. "Let me quote Dr. Steinberg. He just said he predicts we will have determined sex with 100 percent accuracy and eye color with 80 percent accuracy in the next year. Does that give you pause at all?" Rodriguez asked.

"It does. I think he's wrong. I don't think we're going to get to eye color and hair color and freckles for a couple more years. But he's right in principle. We're headed that way. It is going to be possible to pick traits, not because of diseases or avoiding dysfunction, but because somebody has a taste for a particular child or a preference for a particular child," Dr. Caplan said.

"He says that if it is available, why not offer it to his patients? He says he has the obligation as a doctor to do so. Do you agree with that?" Rodriguez asked.

We need more oversight of this industry, and I think this will turn out to be one of the biggest issues in the next 10 [or] 15 years.

Preferences Are Subjective

"I disagree completely. There are really three things to think about. One is, when you move away from diseases, who's to say what's the better trait? Is it better to be red-headed than it is to be brown-haired? Is it better to have freckles or not? Those sorts of things are subjective and in some ways driven by our culture," Caplan said. "Secondly, you're going to have the rich using these technologies, and that's going to advantage them further. It's not going to be something the poor get to do. Lastly, you've got a problem here, why are doctors in this business at all? He said (Dr. Jeff Steinberg), 'I have to serve my patients,' but is this just a cash business where you'd say, you know, 'I want a child with short arms. I want a kid with athletic ability.' Okay. Well, we'll do that. Is everything and anything for sale at the fertility clinic?" Dr. Caplan asked.

The case of Nadya Suleman, who had octuplets, has raised so many debates like this. The doctor who implanted six embryos is being criticized. A lot of people say there should be a law prohibiting that, Rodriguez pointed out.

A Call for Regulation

"Do you think there should be laws prohibiting this?" she asked.

"Absolutely. And the time to start this discussion is right now. For example, I don't think you should get any of these traits offered to you without some counseling so you can think about, is that important to me? Is this really going to make that much difference?" Caplan said.

This can lead to false expectations on children, he explained. The parents may pick a child to be smart, and he or she doesn't succeed, then they become upset because they invested money and didn't get what they want.

"We need more oversight of this industry, and I think this will turn out to be one of the biggest issues in the next 10, 15 years, the extent to which we design our babies and who's going to be able to call the shots, if you will, on whether the technology gets used to do it," Caplan said.

4

Sex Selection Can Lead to Gender Discrimination

Generations Ahead

Generations Ahead is a California-based nonprofit that works to promote the ethical use of genetic technologies by bringing together social justice advocates and organizations.

A truism about sex selection is that when one gender is chosen, the other is deliberately rejected—a choice that has sex discrimination and gender stereotypes at its very heart. This is especially true for ethnic groups that value males more highly than females, such as in various Asian communities where the gender balance has been heavily skewed toward more men and fewer women. While many reproductive rights, feminist, and progressive organizations are deeply troubled by the implications of such blatant gender discrimination, they have been hesitant to oppose sex selection in the United States because they fear that limiting the practice could ultimately undermine a woman's right to terminate a pregnancy. Such groups are working together to educate healthcare providers and the public about the ethical and moral dilemmas inherent in sex selection for nonmedical reasons, and they are working to promote values of gender equality and discourage the practice so that formal regulation becomes unnecessary.

Sex selection is the practice of utilizing medical techniques to have an offspring of a preferred sex. It is a deeply controversial practice that raises important questions about sex

Generations Ahead, *Taking a Stand: Tools for Action on Sex Selection.* Oakland, CA: Generations Ahead, 2010. Used by permission of Generations Ahead.

and gender discrimination and stereotypes, reproductive autonomy, and the ethics of choosing children with specific characteristics. In the United States, many reproductive rights and progressive organizations are troubled by the stereotypes and discrimination that underlie sex selection and the precedent it sets for genetic trait selection, but have hesitated to take a public position opposing sex selection because of concerns about reproductive autonomy and access to abortion.

Compared to many approaches internationally, American policies about sex selection are extremely permissive.

The use of sex selection seems inexorably linked to gendered expectations about what it means to have—or be—a boy or a girl; gender discrimination and the preference for one gender over others; and to a belief that sex and gender can be classified into two distinct male and female forms, rejecting the idea that gender is fluid. However, for as much as reproductive rights advocates would prefer a world without sex selection, they are also deeply concerned that limiting sex selection could implicate abortion rights in the United States and undermine women's reproductive privacy and self-determination. Nonetheless, progressive advocates are being pushed to take a position on sex selection in part because the anti-abortion groups have begun using sex selection as a wedge issue to undermine abortion rights, and in part because of their own pressing concerns about gender discrimination and trait selection. Importantly, some advocates believe that lines can be drawn that uphold abortion rights and discourage sex selection, lines that have been drawn successfully in numerous other countries in the world. Compared to many approaches internationally, American policies about sex selection are extremely permissive.

Increasingly, data in the United States suggest that in Asian-American communities, son preference and the use of sex selection has resulted in more males than females born, specifically when it comes to second and third children in the family. Sex selection is used outside of these communities as well, although there are no data on whether boys or girls are preferred. Outside of the United States, in countries or cultures where abortion is often more accessible and where son preference is a strong tradition, there is stronger evidence of impact on the sex ratio in births—and more active opposition to sex selection from feminist movements and other progressives.

Sex Selection and Reproductive Rights

Conservative anti-abortion groups in the United States are increasingly using sex selection as a wedge issue to attempt to divide progressive communities. The most notable example of this is the "Susan B. Anthony and Frederick Douglass Prenatal Nondiscrimination Act of 2009," Rep. Trent Franks' (R-AZ) proposed legislation to ban sex-selective and "race-selective" abortions. State legislators in Illinois, Pennsylvania, West Virginia, Oklahoma, Michigan, and Minnesota have also either passed or proposed bans on the use of abortion for sex selection, some of which present a real political dilemma: how to oppose gender and race discrimination without aligning with explicitly anti-abortion legislators with no track record on supporting the health and well-being of women and communities of color. Some of the legislators proposing these bills have reached out to the ethnic communities most affected by sex selection and have used the language of gender equality, human rights, and preventing violence against women.

Because of the sometimes competing and conflicting viewpoints at stake in debates surrounding sex selection, and in anticipation of ongoing and future legislative battles, reproductive rights and social justice organizations would be well served to prepare for this complex and politically difficult issue by considering a variety of approaches to sex selection and by articulating a shared set of values and principles.

This brief report on sex selection includes a description of sex selection methods, data on sex selection specifically in the United States, information about current regulation of sex selective practices, some different perspective and viewpoints on the issue, and concludes with some of the values reproductive rights and justice organizations use to take a stand on sex selection.

Conservative anti-abortion groups in the United States are increasingly using sex selection as a wedge issue to attempt to divide progressive communities.

Currently, sex selection techniques may occur before pregnancy or during pregnancy. It is believed that pre-pregnancy methods account for only a small percentage of sex selection procedures in the United States due to their recent introduction, high cost, and the limited number of providers who perform them.

Sex Selection in the United States

There are no official data available on the frequency of pre- and post-pregnancy sex selection in the United States and those who undergo it are often reluctant to discuss it publicly. Some indication of use may be found by examining sex ratios at birth for various populations. Globally, there are 104–107 boys born for every 100 girls, when the sex ratios at birth for a given population fall outside this narrow range, there is strong evidence that sex selection is being done.

Two recent studies relying on 2000 Census data confirm the existence of skewed sex ratios in certain populations in the United States. These studies show evidence of sex selection, and specifically son preference, among Indian-, Chinese-, and Korean-American parents in the United States. In particular, among these populations, although the sex ratio for the oldest child is normal, the sex ratio is heavily male-biased for later births in families with older girls. The sex ratio for second children if the first child was female, was 1.17:1 (male:female), and for the third, the ratio jumped to 1.51:1 if both previous children were female.

Son preference cuts across class lines and seems to have intensified with the trend in Asia and the United States towards having smaller families. It is believed, but not confirmed through research, that the prevalence of son preference in Asian communities in the United States stems from the same reasons for the predominance of sex selection in India, China, and South Korea, reasons such as the elevated social status of men, the ability of sons to carry on the family name and perform certain cultural rituals, men's ability to contribute more to family income, and traditions that require sons to care for aging parents.

Beyond culture, marketing plays a role in the demand for sex selection in the United States. American fertility clinics and doctors offering sex selection actively target Asian-American communities through marketing and advertisements in ethnic newspapers. In one such newspaper, an ad proclaims, "Choosing the sex of your baby a new scientific reality!" Ads targeting the general population have appeared in airline in-flight magazines, asking, "Do you want to choose the gender of your next baby?".

Family balancing refers to the practice of selecting for off-spring of the opposite sex to the children already present in the family.

"Family Balancing"

The use of sex selection is not discernible in overall American birth ratio statistics. Although some clinics offer sex selection for a first or only child, more often they only allow sex selection for "family balancing" or "gender diversity" reasons. Family balancing refers to the practice of selecting for offspring of the opposite sex to the children already present in the family. Microsort, the sperm sorting technique, is offered only for family balancing (and for avoiding sex-linked disease), and many IVF [in vitro fertilization] clinics offer PGD [preimplantation genetic diagnosis] for sex selection only for the same reasons. Defenders of sex selection often state that families in the United States may be as likely to choose girls as boys, although data are not available. Allowing "only" family balancing is not a solution to son preference or gender discrimination. Indeed, the data indicate that Asian families are also practicing family balancing, only selecting for boys in second or third children when earlier children are female.

Professional organizations involved in sex selection are the American Society of Reproductive Medicine (ASRM) and the American College of Obstetricians and Gynecologists (ACOG).

Regulation of Sex Selection

Sex selection—other than to avoid sex-linked diseases—has been banned in most industrialized countries, with the United States as the notable exception. In the United States, there is virtually no federal or state regulation of sex selection, although voluntary professional guidelines do exist. Even though federal laws regulate certain aspects of assisted reproductive technology (ART), there is no regulation of sex selection specifically. State regulation of ART is likewise very limited. Legislators in Illinois, Pennsylvania, West Virginia, Oklahoma, Michigan, and Minnesota have proposed or enacted legislation to ban sex selective abortions.

Professional organizations involved in sex selection are the American Society for Reproductive Medicine (ASRM) and the

American College of Obstetricians and Gynecologists (ACOG). Ethical opinions and guidelines issued by ASRM and ACOG are voluntary, although these organizations could enforce their rules against their members by taking away their membership or otherwise disciplining them publicly, something they have done very infrequently to date. The ASRM Ethics Committee has published several opinions on sex selection. One opinion focuses on PGD, and states that among infertile patients using IVF for infertility, the addition of PGD solely for sex selection "should not be encouraged" and use of IVF and PGD solely for sex selection where infertility is not an issue "should be discouraged." The Ethics Committee also recommended that if pre-pregnancy techniques, particularly sperm sorting, were found to be safe and effective, doctors should be able to offer them to couples for family balancing, as long as certain conditions such as informed consent are met. Both guidelines express the concern that sex selection may perpetuate sex discrimination, gender role expectations and stereotypes.

ACOG's Committee on Ethics has concluded that sex selection for family balancing is inappropriate. However, the Committee also held that when procedures are undergone for reasons other than discerning the sex of the fetus but will nonetheless reveal the fetus' sex, this information should not be withheld from the pregnant woman if she requests it, as "this information legally and ethically belongs to [her]." ACOG has declared that "[n]o current technique for prefertilization sex selection [including sperm sorting] has been shown to be reliable."

Differing Views on Sex Selection

Those who advocate for discouraging or restricting sex selection may be concerned with any one or combination of the following concerns. That sex selection:

1. will affect sex ratios in the population,

2. stems from gender inequality and discrimination,

3. perpetuates a view that gender is binary rather than fluid,

4. could include coercion, domestic violence or a lack of informed consent,

5. sets a precedent for allowing trait selection, and/ or

6. encourages the pursuit of "perfect" children that will negatively impact people with disabilities.

Those who do not support restricting sex selection may share some of these views but worry more that restrictions would have implications for privacy and abortion rights.

Under a traditional pro-choice perspective women should have an unfettered choice in whether or not to obtain an abortion, and any inquiry or second-guessing of a woman's reasons violates her autonomy and is politically dangerous in that it invites opposition to other reasons for abortion as well. *Roe v. Wade* grounded the right to abortion in a woman's right to privacy and that right protects a woman's right to choose an abortion based on any reason—or for no specific reason at all. It is not clear whether the Supreme Court would find legislative bans or other restrictions on sex selection con-stitutional. Recent Supreme Court cases have held that the state may place limits on a woman's right to obtain abortions as long as they are not overly burdensome. Narrowly defined limits, such as 24-hour waiting periods and mandatory sono-grams, have passed constitutional muster. The Supreme Court could find that sex selection perpetuates—or is equivalent to—discrimination against women, and that preventing dis-crimination against women is a legitimate state interest that overrides the right to obtain an abortion.

A Preference for Sons

Among international and global feminists the primary con-cern is that in many countries most sex selection is done for son preference. Sex selection for son preference is a stark reminder that gender discrimination still shapes the life experience of millions of women and girls. Coercion and violence are also of concern; women in some communities who do not bear sons may be coerced into using sex selection or subjected to domestic violence and other forms of discrimination for not having a son. However, banning sex selective abortions could place a significant burden on women, pushing the procedures underground and limiting access to abortion. Many countries have been able to discourage and regulate sex selection and still support access to abortion. They focus efforts to decrease gender discrimination and sex selection on broader initiatives to increase the resources, protections, and rights of women.

Sex selection ignores the fact that gender is not binary but fluid, reflecting how a person feels, chooses to express themselves, and is perceived.

Social vs. Medical Reasons

The motivations for utilizing different sex selective techniques are often divided into medical reasons (to prevent sex-linked genetic disorders) and social reasons. While undergoing sex selection for medical reasons is often not contested, disability rights advocates argue that the use of technologies to select for fetuses free of medical concerns or conditions can be a "social," not "medical," use. The decision to eliminate embryos or fetuses based on a genetic condition may both reflect and perpetuate society's stereotypes and biases against disability.

Allowing sex selection for either medical reasons or parental preferences is an example of permitting parents to choose traits of their future children. Although the ability to select embryos and fetuses for complex traits is far off scientifically, undoubtedly some companies will market such tests to parents regardless of their actual scientific soundness. For some, sex selection, as well as other techniques allowing parents to choose embryos and fetuses with specific traits, characteristics or genetic conditions, falls outside acceptable reproductive rights concerns of deciding when to have a child and lands in murkier territory of whether the right to choose includes or should include deciding which types of children are acceptable or unacceptable.

The use of sex selective techniques is premised on the belief that the child will have certain stereotypical gendered attributes and/or identity. Sex selection ignores the fact that gender is not binary but fluid, reflecting how a person feels, chooses to express themselves, and is perceived. Lesbian, gay, bisexual, transgender and queer (LGBTQ) communities are also particularly concerned about sex selection's perpetuation of gender binary and sexual stereotypes.

Ultimately, sex selection is the gateway issue to an even more complex array of issues related to reproductive technologies and genetic trait selection.

Reproductive Justice Concerns

Within the reproductive justice movement major concerns with sex selection relate to the discrimination against and mistreatment of women and girls, specifically Asian women and girls in the United States, and the reinforcement of gender stereotypes and binaries. Reproductive justice perspectives consider the intersection of race, ethnicity, class, culture, sexual orientation, and economics. Seeking to protect gender and racial equality and reproductive rights, they are proponents of discouraging sex selection and trait selection at the same time as protecting access to abortion. Given the experience of other feminists around the world, they believe that the focus of this work should be on changing social norms and culture while fighting for policies that promote gender and race equity.

Creating a Demand for Sex Selection

Complex factors—including sex discrimination, sexual stereotypes and gender binary assumptions, aggressive advertising by sex selection providers, desire for small families, and cultural forces—combine to create a market for the practice of sex selection technologies. The challenge is to address these gender equality issues while protecting abortion rights. In April 2009, Generations Ahead, NAPAWF [National Asian Pacific American Women's Forum], SisterSong and the Center for Reproductive Rights brought together more than 25 reproductive health, rights and justice organizations with some South Asian domestic violence prevention organizations to clarify their values on sex selection and identify possible actions to take on this issue. Participants declared that they supported race and gender equality and were concerned about protecting abortion access. They cited four principles that would inform their organizations in developing positions on sex selection: a strong pro-choice position, promoting and respecting human rights, centering the voices of those most affected, and the intersection of race, gender, sexuality and immigration concerns.

Shortly after this convening, the Center for Reproductive Rights (CRR) developed a statement of policies and principles on sex selective abortion. Framed as an issue of gender-based discrimination that needed to be condemned and addressed by both government and private actors, CRR opposes any bans on sex selective abortions citing that they: are ineffective, threaten the lives and health of women by making abortion harder to obtain, undermine women's autonomy, and are part of an anti-choice agenda.

Shared Principles and Values

Most communities want to see less demand for and use of sex selection in the United States and around the world. At a time when anti-choice policymakers have seized on sex selection as a potential wedge issue to use to divide progressive and social justice organizations, it is critically important to remain focused on that shared goal. The most critical first step is that reproductive health, rights and justice organizations articulate shared principles and values concerning sex selection. Next, public education and media campaigns, as well as organized efforts to work with health professionals and community leaders, can promote gender equality, diminish stereotypes about sex and gender, and raise the social status of women and girls while working with allies across social justice movements. Ultimately, sex selection is the gateway issue to an even more complex array of issues related to reproductive technologies and genetic trait selection. How well we do in taking a stand on sex selection might lay the foundation for how we approach this next generation of issues.

5

Sex Selection Will Not Lead to Gender Discrimination

Edgar Dahl

Edgar Dahl is a spokesman for the German Society for Reproductive Medicine. He is a contributor to Ethical Technologies, *a project of the Institute for Ethics and Emerging Technologies, a Connecticut-based nonprofit that works to stimulate and support constructive study of ethical issues connected with today's powerful emerging technologies.*

The US Food and Drug Administration (FDA) has banned the MicroSort sex selection procedure from being used for "family balancing," the practice of selecting sperm of one sex or the other to achieve a mix of male and female children. The FDA's decision was based on the argument that the technology has no public health benefit. Nothing could be further from reality, and the case for approving such a procedure is stronger than that for cosmetic procedures, such as liposuction. In truth, the perceived problem with MicroSort is an ethical one, but that too is misguided. Most Americans who want to select the sex of their children are not doing so to favor one gender over another but rather to round out their family so that it includes children of both sexes. American parents do not systematically choose one sex over the other, and banning sex selection in the US will do nothing to address the phenomenon of skewed sex ratios in countries like China and India. Such a shift in gender patterns is not a danger in this country, and fears of negative social consequences from the impact of "designer babies" are patently unfounded.

Edgar Dahl, "FDA Bans Gender Selection Procedure," *Ethical Technology*, May 17, 2011. Used by permission.

The American Food and Drug Administration [FDA] has required the Genetics and IVF Center in Fairfax, Virginia, to stop offering MicroSort for family balancing. Currently, the procedure is available only for "couples attempting to prevent sex-linked or sex-limited disease."

MicroSort is a device that allows the separation of X- from Y-bearing sperm. Thanks to MicroSort, more than one thousand couples have been able to have a baby of their choice. These couples include those who were at risk of transmitting a sex-linked genetic disorder as well as those who, say, after having three or four boys were longing for a girl.

Why is the FDA preventing the Genetics and IVF Institute from offering gender selection for family balancing? Well, the only reason given was that there is no "public health benefit" in offering gender selection for non-medical purposes.

Pardon my French, but I think this is total B.S.!

The only thing the FDA has a right to be concerned with is the safety and efficacy of the procedure. And by the FDA's own admission, MicroSort *is* safe and effective. Whether or not it meets public health needs is, frankly, none of the FDA's business. After all, there are countless pharmaceutical drugs and medical procedures which fail to meet "public health needs."

Justifying Sex Selection

Thus, whatever we think of the ethics of gender selection, one thing should be clear: if cosmetic surgery, such as liposuction, is worthy of approval, gender selection should be worthy of approval. In fact, the case for gender selection is much *stronger* than the case for liposuction.

Just as a woman may suffer from being overweight, a woman may suffer from not being able to have the daughter she was longing for all her life. Moreover, a woman not having a flat stomach DOES have alternatives while a woman not having a daughter DOES NOT. The chubby woman does not have to turn to medicine for help. In most cases, she can simply remedy herself by sports and diets. The daughterless woman, however, has no choice but to turn to medicine. And the FDA *knows* this.

So why doesn't it just come out and tell the truth? Why can't the FDA just be honest and say: MicroSort does not pose a medical problem, it poses an ETHICAL problem. Gender selection through sperm sorting may be safe and reliable, but it is widely seen as "immoral."

It would be justified to regulate gender selection if there was a clear and present danger of distorting our gender ratio.

Indeed, sex selection for non-medical reasons makes a lot of people uneasy. They somehow FEEL it is wrong. Even if they can't quite put their finger on it, they just KNOW it is something we shouldn't be doing.

For lack of an argument, they often claim that it is "unnatural." Well, one doesn't have to be a philosopher to see that it is entirely irrelevant whether an action is natural or unnatural. My personal hero, the Scottish philosopher David Hume, once stated that although something may be natural or unnatural, that doesn't settle the question whether it is moral or immoral. This, he suggested, remains an open question.

It's easy to see Hume's point. Transplanting a heart to save a man's life is certainly UNNATURAL. But who would claim that it is THEREFORE morally wrong?

The same applies to the notion that gender selection is "playing God." By inoculating children against smallpox or other diseases they could die of, we are certainly "playing God." But does this render all inoculations or vaccinations immoral? I don't think so.

Like the notion of gender selection being "unnatural," so the notion of gender selection as "playing God" is not a considered response, let alone an argument. It is simply a gut reaction.

No Clear and Present Danger

What would be a valid objection? I'm inclined to say: it would be justified to regulate gender selection if there was a clear and present danger of distorting our gender ratio.

We have all heard about countries like India, China, or South Korea where women are outnumbered by men. Nobel Prize winning economist Amartya Sen once famously wrote about Asia's missing women. In their book *Bare Branches*, political scientists Valerie Hudson and Andrea den Boer point out that China soon will be faced with a "hoodlum army of 30 million bachelors" threatening the country's security.

I don't want to get into a debate about Asia's demographic problems except to state that Chinese and Indian women do have religious and financial incentives for preferring boys over girls—incentives which are absent in America and the rest of the Western world.

Over the last ten years, I have surveyed the general population, pregnant women, and IVF [in vitro fertilization] couples in Germany, Britain, and the United States as well as in Pakistan, Jordan, and Trinidad & Tobago. The results for Germany, Britain and the United States are pretty much the same: First, there is no preference for children of a particular gender anymore. Second, if there is any preference at all, it is a preference for having children of both sexes. And third, only a small minority can envisage employing, undergoing and paying for gender selection to ensure the birth of a child of a particular sex. For example, in the US only 8% and in Germany only 6% of the general population could imagine using MicroSort.

Running the Numbers

Data from so-called "gender clinics" support these findings. The overwhelming majority of couples seeking gender selection—more than 90%—are couples who already have three or more children of the same sex longing to have at least one child of the opposite sex. When compared, couples with three or more boys are more likely to turn to a gender clinic than couples with three or more girls. And last but not least, it is typically the woman who initiates the contact to a fertility specialist.

How many children are already born through social gender selection in the US? We don't know! Still, we are in the position to make an educated guess. It is said that about 1% of children in the US are now conceived through in-vitro fertilization. This means that out of the four million children born every year, about forty thousand are "test-tube babies." If, as has been claimed, 5% of IVF cycles are now combined with PGD (preimplantation genetic diagnosis) for the sole purpose of social gender selection, we are talking about two thousand sex-selected children.

Preventing American couples from choosing the gender of their children will not change the gender ratio of India.

Two thousand out of four million children is almost nothing. It's like a drop in the ocean. Even if this number were to grow by a factor of ten—which is conceivable as social gender selection may become more and more acceptable—we are still talking about only twenty thousand out of four million children per year. Given that these children are not always of one particular gender, but of both genders, selected to balance the composition of individual American families, there is no reason at all to be concerned about the gender ratio.

While a socially disruptive distortion of the natural gender ratio is not a problem in Western countries, it surely *is* a problem in some Asian countries. Hence it doesn't come as a surprise that a few authors have called for a worldwide ban on social gender selection.

US Prohibition Would Not Help Global Problem

However, does the practice of social gender selection in, say, India really justify prohibiting social gender selection in the United States? The simple answer is: Most certainly not!

First, preventing American couples from choosing the gender of their children will not change the gender ratio of India. Second, even if it is only meant to "send a message," it is simply naive to assume that Indian families will appreciate our gesture, well-meaning as it may be. As long as there are religious and economic incentives within a culture for preferring boys over girls, our moral plea will fall on deaf ears. Third, and most importantly, denying American couples the opportunity to have a daughter because Indian couples have killed theirs would amount to punishing the innocent. There is no moral justification *whatsoever* for punishing the people of one country for actions committed by the people of another.

Almost all couples seeking gender selection are simply motivated by the desire to have at least one child of each sex.

Another objection to MicroSort claims that gender selection constitutes gender discrimination. While this claim may apply to, say, infanticide, it certainly does NOT apply to MicroSort. Discrimination is the violation of human or civil rights on the sole basis of race, gender, or religion. Thus it can only apply to already existing people, not to mere gametes, such as sperms or eggs. Entities that do not yet exist and do not yet have rights simply cannot be discriminated against.

Concerns About Sexism

Another frequently advanced objection claims that gender selection is "sexist." Some feminist philosophers even went so far as to call gender selection "the original sexist sin." Gender selection, they argue, is deeply wrong because it makes "the most basic judgement about the worth of a human being rest first and foremost on its sex."

However, this argument is deeply flawed. It is simply false that people who choose the gender of their children are motivated by the sexist belief that one gender is more "valuable" than the other. As already mentioned, almost all couples seeking gender selection are simply motivated by the desire to have at least one child of each sex. If this desire is based on any beliefs at all, it is based on the quite defensible assumption that raising a girl is different from raising a boy, but certainly not on the preposterous idea that one gender is "superior" to the other.

A further objection concerns the welfare of children born as a result of gender selection. Thus, it has been argued that gender-selected children may be expected to behave in certain gender-specific ways and risk being resented if they fail to do so. Although it cannot be completely ruled out, it is highly unlikely that children conceived after MicroSort are going to suffer from unreasonable parental expectations. Couples seeking gender selection to ensure the birth of a daughter are very well aware that they can expect a girl, not some Angelina Jolie; and couples going for a son know perfectly well they can expect a boy, not some Brad Pitt.

A Slippery Slope?

Last but not least, there is the widely popular objection that gender selection is the first step down a road that will inevitably lead to the creation of "designer babies." Once we allow parents to choose the gender of their children, we will soon find ourselves allowing them to choose their eye color, their height, or their intelligence.

This slippery slope objection calls for three remarks. First, it is not an argument against gender selection *per se*, but only against its alleged consequences.

Second, and more importantly, it is based on the assumption that we are simply incapable of preventing the alleged consequences from happening. However, this view is utterly untenable. It's perfectly possible to draw a legal line permitting some forms of selection and prohibiting others. Thus, if selection for gender is morally acceptable but selection for, say, intelligence is not, the former can be allowed and the latter not.

And third, the slippery slope argument presumes that sliding down the slope is going to have devastating social effects. However, in the case of selecting offspring traits, this is far from obvious. What is so terrifying about the idea that some parents may be foolish enough to spend their hard-earned money on genetic technologies just to ensure their child will be born with big brown eyes or black curly hair? I am sorry, but I cannot see that this would be the end of civilization as we know it.

6

Women Should Have the Right to Choose the Sex of Their Children

Christine Hicks

Christine Hicks writes a blog under the pen name "Oryoki Bowl" at OpenSalon.com, a social content website hosted by Salon.

Having an abortion because of the sex of a fetus has recently been made illegal in Arizona, and there is a push for other states to follow suit with similar laws. Because all children who are brought into this world should be wanted ones, women should not have to justify or explain their reasons for wanting to terminate a specific pregnancy. A woman's right to choose should be protected, regardless of her reason. Sex-selective abortions in other countries are troubling, but there is a lot of logic behind the practice in the context of cultural conditions; in many cases, the alternative is giving birth to a girl child who will face a higher likelihood of abuse and neglect, infant mortality, starvation, exploitation, human trafficking, slavery, and even murder. Which is worse: to live a grim and horrible life or not to have lived at all?

Arizona recently passed the first law in the nation that explicitly forbids abortion for the purposes of selecting against race and gender. I found out about this with the recent flurry of email activity from Planned Parenthood, signing petitions to ask our Governor to stop these laws from being

Christine Hicks, "An Unpopular Choice: Sex Selection and Abortion," opensalon.com, April 6, 2011. Used by permission of the author.

passed. Although the law clearly forbids abortion for these reasons, it is not clearly an issue as it is in places such as India and China. We have no reason to think this is an issue in the US, but who's to say?

Meanwhile in India, their census indicated a huge decline in the balance of girls born to boys born. This can only be explained by sex selective abortion. Although banned in India, this is a common practice and it is well known that it occurs around the time that a gender can be determined via ultrasound. News reports recently talked of dozens of female fetuses in the garbage behind such a clinic. Reports last year [2010] in China spoke of the dozens of aborted female fetuses found in the sewage behind a hospital and polluting a local creek. History shows us a widespread practice of female infanticide. Male children can always get another wife from some other tribe, or can make good soldiers to protect the elders and their wives.

All Children Should Be Wanted

I'm a pro-choice woman, and while I am saddened by the practice of gender biased abortion, I don't want to criminalize it for several reasons. I believe a woman has the right to have an abortion when she does not want to give birth to that particular child. I don't want her to have to explain herself, or justify why. All abortions are unwanted children, for whatever reasons the parent or parents have chosen to abort. I am totally for having only wanted children born into this world.

In the natural world, a mammal may choose to save a male offspring over a female.

In the natural world, there are pros and cons to having a daughter. Depending on the species, it can be very costly to have a daughter. As with humans. Daughters can only have so many children, usually one at a time, and invest an incredible amount of physical energy and time into their gestation, birth and upbringing of their child. They are not available again for more reproduction for a long period of time. If traditional means of breastfeeding and natural sleep cycles followed, a female human may not be able to get pregnant again for months or years after a birth. There are high rates of morbidity and mortality with pregnancy, birth and the perinatal period. A pregnant and breastfeeding woman needs a lot of support.

The Genetic Imperative

Meanwhile, a son can get dozens of women pregnant within a short period of time, and invests as much as he cares to. The genetic investment is the same, but the physical and energetic expenditure is pretty low. Of course, fighting for access to females (like in war) can be costly. Local laws about marriage and access to females based on age and wealth can impact the amount of reproduction going on. Thus, marriage laws are created to ensure that males have access to at least one female with whom he can procreate (and recreate). This keeps men from constantly fighting each other. Most societies have some version of prostitution, for the non reproducing male, or ritualized abuse of children. In the natural world, a mammal may choose to save a male offspring over a female, because that male can deliver a lot of sperm in a short period of time. Remember, reproduction is about genetics, and genetics are selfish. Altruism is not only very rare, it rarely happens outside of genetically related clans. Even the movie *Sophie's Choice* addresses this, the unconscious choice many of us would make without realizing why.

In the traditional world, a costly daughter must be protected from male predators in the family and strangers. This takes time and resources. A male can produce more labor that results in income, or become a soldier or priest, but a male cannot have an accidental and costly pregnancy (obviously he can cause one, but marriage laws protect men against that as well). In countries where parents can possibly afford to raise one or two children (if they are allowed more than one), a son is almost always desired. He has the genetic potential to parent dozens of children, he has the economic potential to support his parents, and he cannot bring home an extra mouth to feed the way a woman can. These are similar rationales behind why daughters-in-law are often treated so poorly, being starved, beaten, set on fire and killed. They must bring a dowry to pay for their own care while living and serving in their mother in law's home.

Which Is Worse?

As China and India have their own reasons behind gender selection abortion, consider the alternative. A girl child being born unwanted. She will face a higher likelihood of abuse, infant death, starvation, sexual exploitation, human trafficking (on the rise all around the world, parents selling off their daughters for sex trafficking). She is more likely to be sold into slavery for domestic exploitation. She is more likely to be abused and enslaved at every level of her life, if she is born. She is more likely to be killed.

It should be illegal to deny anyone an abortion based on their reasons for having one.

We cry out against abortions for the reasons of eugenics, such as the recent spate of anti-abortion blather crying genocide of the African American Community. Considering that in the United States, the issue is not one of gender or racial identity of the fetus—but perhaps of the mother—the laws of economics and actual natural selection are still at play. The likely reason more African American women have abortions is due to lack of access to comprehensive sex education at an appropriate age, lack of access to reasonable birth control at the age of sexual activity onset, and perhaps other factors that coincide with the higher rates of low economic status. These women are making very smart decisions when they choose to delay motherhood in favor of having more access to economic freedom.

Arizona used to have a loophole in abortion law, for instances when the mother was white and the father was black. Naturally it was presumed a product of rape (especially if you define all interracial sex as illegal and therefore rape). AZ might have had similar miscegenation rules like the rest of the country, as to interracial reproduction and marriage.

I am not applauding the passage of this law, because I don't believe it addresses a real problem. I think it should be illegal to deny anyone an abortion based on their reasons for having one. If you don't want to give birth and raise this child, with love, in a safe environment, that is an excellent reason for abortion. Most women would have preferred to not have gotten pregnant in the first place.

I can't possibly see how forcing anyone to have a child that is undesired will result in raising respect for women.

The Cycle Will Continue

China and India are facing a woman shortage, and this will continue as time passes and the available males can not find suitable partners for marriage and reproduction. What will happen? For one, there will be an even greater fall in birthrates, continuing the population control issues both face. Eligible females will have more value, and many other women will be forced into sex trafficking to be shared with the ineligible men. Trafficked women will continue to have abortions, and married women will likely continue to select for sons. This will make the imbalance continue. And it is unsustainable for the future. Right now, plummeting birth rates in countries such as Japan and Italy are making lawmakers offer money to families to reproduce. Eventually, in places like that, there will be more showdowns between women, men and the law for the right to contraception, the right to abortion and the right to choose.

I can't possibly see how forcing anyone to have a child that is undesired will result in raising respect for women. What does raise respect for women? Education, limited reproduction, and laws that punish men for physical and sexual abuse. As the remaining men will have to fight each other for access to a wife, different wars will break out, different laws will emerge, and a change in society will eventually happen. Will it lead to more female empowerment? Not too likely, at this point. Does reducing unwanted children in the world reduce suffering? I believe it does.

7

Sex Selection Can Lead to Trait-Based Eugenics

Gautam Naik

Journalist Gautam Naik writes about health, medicine, and emerging technologies for the Wall Street Journal, *a daily newspaper.*

Technology that has long been used to detect life-threatening diseases in embryos has developed to the point where it can be used to build babies that have specific physical traits, such as a particular gender or eye or hair color. Critics fear that designing humans with specific traits—at the exclusion of other traits—will create new eugenics-based biases and sources of discrimination. The even bigger fear is that the technology could also eventually be used to select for such things as intelligence or athletic ability. One fertility clinic that hopes to offer various trait-based selection services, however, sees it as nothing more than another type of "cosmetic medicine"—simply another choice that can be offered to reproductive health consumers. The scientist who controls the most reliable method for trait selection refuses to let it be used for such nonmedical purposes, however, underscoring how controversial and divisive the issue is even within the medical community itself.

Want a daughter with blond hair, green eyes and pale skin?

A Los Angeles [California] clinic says it will soon help couples select both gender and physical traits in a baby when

Gautam Naik, "A Baby, Please. Blond, Freckles—Hold the Colic," *The Wall Street Journal*, February 12, 2009. Used by permission.

they undergo a form of fertility treatment. The clinic, Fertility Institutes, says it has received "half a dozen" requests for the service, which is based on a procedure called pre-implantation genetic diagnosis, or PGD.

Pre-selecting cosmetic traits in a baby is no longer the stuff of science fiction.

While PGD has long been used for the medical purpose of averting life-threatening diseases in children, the science behind it has quietly progressed to the point that it could potentially be used to create designer babies. It isn't clear that Fertility Institutes can yet deliver on its claims of trait selection. But the growth of PGD, unfettered by any state or federal regulations in the U.S., has accelerated genetic knowledge swiftly enough that pre-selecting cosmetic traits in a baby is no longer the stuff of science fiction.

"It's technically feasible and it can be done," says Mark Hughes, a pioneer of the PGD process and director of Genesis Genetics Institute, a large fertility laboratory in Detroit [Michigan]. However, he adds that "no legitimate lab would get into it and, if they did, they'd be ostracized."

But Fertility Institutes disagrees. "This is cosmetic medicine," says Jeff Steinberg, director of the clinic that is advertising gender and physical trait selection on its Web site. "Others are frightened by the criticism but we have no problems with it."

PGD is a technique whereby a three-day-old embryo, consisting of about six cells, is tested in a lab to see if it carries a particular genetic disease. Embryos free of that disease are implanted in the mother's womb. Introduced in the 1990s, it has allowed thousands of parents to avoid passing on deadly disorders to their children.

Should Parents Be Allowed to Choose the Sex of Their Children?

Selecting for Cosmetic Traits

But PGD is starting to be used to target less-serious disorders or certain characteristics—such as a baby's gender—that aren't medical conditions. The next controversial step is to select physical traits for cosmetic reasons.

"If we're going to produce children who are claimed to be superior because of their particular genes, we risk introducing new sources of discrimination" in society, says Marcy Darnovsky, associate executive director of the Center for Genetics and Society, a nonprofit public interest group in Oakland, Calif. If people use the method to select babies who are more likely to be tall, the thinking goes, then people could effectively be enacting their biases against short people.

In a recent U.S. survey of 999 people who sought genetic counseling, a majority said they supported prenatal genetic tests for the elimination of certain serious diseases. The survey found that 56% supported using them to counter blindness and 75% for mental retardation.

If we're going to produce children who are claimed to be superior because of their particular genes, we risk introducing new sources of discrimination.

More provocatively, about 10% of respondents said they would want genetic testing for athletic ability, while another 10% voted for improved height. Nearly 13% backed the approach to select for superior intelligence, according to the survey conducted by researchers at the New York University School of Medicine.

Many Factors Involved

There are significant hurdles to any form of genetic enhancement. Most human traits are controlled by multiple genetic factors, and knowledge about their complex workings, though

56

accelerating, is incomplete. And traits such as athleticism and intelligence are affected not just by DNA, but by environmental factors that cannot be controlled in a lab.

While many countries have banned the use of PGD for gender selection, it is permitted in the U.S. In 2006, a survey by the Genetics and Public Policy Center at Johns Hopkins University found that 42% of 137 PGD clinics offered a gender-selection service.

About 10% of respondents said they would want genetic testing for athletic ability, while another 10% voted for improved height. Nearly 13% backed the approach to select for superior intelligence.

The science of PGD has steadily expanded its scope, often in contentious ways. Embryo screening, for example, is sometimes used to create a genetically matched "savior sibling"—a younger sister or brother whose healthy cells can be harvested to treat an older sibling with a serious illness.

It also is increasingly used to weed out embryos at risk of genetic diseases—such as breast cancer—that could be treated, or that might not strike a person later in life. In 2007, the Bridge Centre fertility clinic in London [United Kingdom] screened embryos so that a baby wouldn't suffer from a serious squint that afflicted the father.

"Negative Enhancement"

Instead of avoiding some conditions, the technique also may have been used to select an embryo likely to have the same disease or disability, such as deafness, that affects the parents. The Johns Hopkins survey found that 3% of PGD clinics had provided this service, sometimes described as "negative enhancement." Groups who support this approach argue, for example, that a deaf child born to a deaf couple is better suited to participating in the parents' shared culture. So far, however, no single clinic has been publicly identified as offering this service.

Like several genetic diseases, cosmetic traits are correlated with a large number of DNA variations or markers—known as single nucleotide polymorphisms, or SNPs—that work in combination. A new device called the microarray, a small chip coated with DNA sequences, can simultaneously analyze many more spots on the chromosomes.

In October 2007, scientists from deCode Genetics of Iceland published a paper in *Nature Genetics* pinpointing various SNPs that influence skin, eye and hair color, based on samples taken from people in Iceland and the Netherlands. Along with related genes discovered earlier, "the variants described in this report enable prediction of pigmentation traits based upon an individual's DNA," the company said. Such data, the researchers said, could be useful for teasing out the biology of skin and eye disease and for forensic DNA analysis.

Kari Stefansson, chief executive of deCode, points out that such a test will only provide a certain level of probability that a child will have blond hair or green eyes, not an absolute guarantee. He says: "I vehemently oppose the use of these discoveries for tailor-making children." In the long run, he adds, such a practice would "decrease human diversity, and that's dangerous."

In theory, these data could be used to analyze the DNA of an embryo and determine whether it was more likely to give rise to a baby of a particular hair, skin or eye tint. (The test won't work on other ethnicities such as Asians or Africans because key pigmentation markers for those groups haven't yet been identified.)

Interpreting DNA

For trait selection, a big hurdle is getting enough useful DNA material from the embryo. In a typical PGD procedure, a single cell is removed from a six-cell embryo and tested for the relevant genes or SNPs. It's relatively easy to check and eliminate diseases such as cystic fibrosis that are linked to a single malfunctioning gene. But to read the larger number of SNP markers associated with complex ailments such as diabetes, or traits like hair color, there often isn't enough high-quality genetic material.

William Kearns, a medical geneticist and director of the Shady Grove Center for Preimplantation Genetics in Rockville, Md., says he has made headway in cracking the problem. In a presentation made at a November [2008] meeting of the American Society of Human Genetics in Philadelphia [Pennsylvania], he described how he had managed to amplify the DNA available from a single embryonic cell to identify complex diseases and also certain physical traits.

Of 42 embryos tested, Dr. Kearns said he had enough data to identify SNPs that relate to northern European skin, hair and eye pigmentation in 80% of the samples. (A patent for Dr. Kearns' technique is pending; the test data are unpublished and have yet to be reviewed by other scientists.)

Vying for Technologies

Dr. Kearns' talk attracted the attention of Dr. Steinberg, the head of Fertility Institutes, which already offers PGD for gender selection. The clinic had hoped to collaborate with Dr. Kearns to offer trait selection as well. In December [2008], the clinic's Web site announced that couples who signed up for embryo screening would soon be able to make "a pre-selected choice of gender, eye color, hair color and complexion, along with screening for potentially lethal diseases."

Dr. Kearns says he is firmly against the idea of using PGD to select nonmedical traits. He plans to offer his PGD amplification technique to fertility clinics for medical purposes such as screening for complex disorders, but won't let it be used for physical trait selection. "I'm not going to do designer babies," says Dr. Kearns. "I won't sell my soul for a dollar." A spokes-woman for Dr. Steinberg said: "The relationship between them is very amicable, and this center looks forward to working with Dr. Kearns."

For trait selection, Dr. Steinberg is now betting on a new approach for screening embryos. It involves taking cells from an embryo at day five of its development, compared with typical PGD, which uses cells from day three. The method potentially allows more cells to be obtained, leading to a more reliable diagnosis of the embryo.

Trait selection in babies "is a service," says Dr. Steinberg. "We intend to offer it soon."

8

Sex Selection Leads to Gendercide in China and India

The Economist

The Economist is a weekly international news and business magazine.

Because of a strong and persistent cultural preference for male children and a modern desire for small families, birth ratios in countries like China and India are heavily skewed toward boys; as many as 120 boys are being born for every 100 girls, and in some areas the ratio is even higher. While in the past unwanted girls were often killed or abandoned once they were born, modern technology now allows prospective parents to learn the sex of their baby very early in a pregnancy. The result is that girl babies are being aborted in staggering numbers, wildly skewing the birth ratios. Such sex selective abortion amounts to a "gendercide," in which millions of women are simply missing from society—a disparity that has severe social consequences. Countries where sex selective abortion is prevalent must work to find ways to raise the value of girls and women in their societies so that this gross gender imbalance can be reversed.

Imagine you are one half of a young couple expecting your first child in a fast-growing, poor country. You are part of the new middle class; your income is rising; you want a small family. But traditional *mores* hold sway around you, most im-

"The War on Baby Girls—Killed, Aborted or Neglected, at Least 100m Girls Have Disappeared—and the Number Is Rising," *The Economist*, March 4, 2010. Used by permission.

portant in the preference for sons over daughters. Perhaps hard physical labour is still needed for the family to make its living. Perhaps only sons may inherit land. Perhaps a daughter is deemed to join another family on marriage and you want someone to care for you when you are old. Perhaps she needs a dowry.

China alone stands to have as many unmarried young men . . . as the entire population of young men in America.

Now imagine that you have had an ultrasound scan; it costs $12, but you can afford that. The scan says the unborn child is a girl. You yourself would prefer a boy; the rest of your family clamours for one. You would never dream of killing a baby daughter, as they do out in the villages. But an abortion seems different. What do you do?

The Consequences of Choice

For millions of couples, the answer is: abort the daughter, try for a son. In China and northern India more than 120 boys are being born for every 100 girls. Nature dictates that slightly more males are born than females to offset boys' greater susceptibility to infant disease. But nothing on this scale.

For those who oppose abortion, this is mass murder. For those such as this newspaper, who think abortion should be "safe, legal and rare" (to use Bill Clinton's phrase), a lot depends on the circumstances, but the cumulative consequence for societies of such individual actions is catastrophic. China alone stands to have as many unmarried young men—"bare branches", as they are known—as the entire population of young men in America. In any country rootless young males spell trouble; in Asian societies, where marriage and children are the recognised routes into society, single men are almost like outlaws. Crime rates, bride trafficking, sexual violence, even female suicide rates are all rising and will rise further as the lopsided generations reach their maturity.

It is no exaggeration to call this gendercide. Women are missing in the millions—aborted, killed, neglected to death. In 1990 an Indian economist, Amartya Sen, put the number at 100m [million]; the toll is higher now. The crumb of comfort is that countries can mitigate the hurt, and that one, South Korea, has shown the worst can be avoided. Others need to learn from it if they are to stop the carnage.

The Dearth and Death of Little Sisters

Most people know China and northern India have unnaturally large numbers of boys. But few appreciate how bad the problem is, or that it is rising. In China the imbalance between the sexes was 108 boys to 100 girls for the generation born in the late 1980s; for the generation of the early 2000s, it was 124 to 100. In some Chinese provinces the ratio is an unprecedented 130 to 100. The destruction is worst in China but has spread far beyond. Other East Asian countries, including Taiwan and Singapore, former communist states in the western Balkans and the Caucasus, and even sections of America's population (Chinese- and Japanese-Americans, for example): all these have distorted sex ratios. Gendercide exists on almost every continent. It affects rich and poor; educated and illiterate; Hindu, Muslim, Confucian and Christian alike.

It is no exaggeration to call this gendercide. Women are missing in the millions—aborted, killed, neglected to death.

Wealth does not stop it. Taiwan and Singapore have open, rich economies. Within China and India the areas with the worst sex ratios are the richest, best-educated ones. And China's one-child policy can only be part of the problem, given that so many other countries are affected.

In fact the destruction of baby girls is a product of three forces: the ancient preference for sons; a modern desire for smaller families; and ultrasound scanning and other technologies that identify the sex of a fetus. In societies where four or six children were common, a boy would almost certainly come along eventually; son preference did not need to exist at the expense of daughters. But now couples want two children—or, as in China, are allowed only one—they will sacrifice unborn daughters to their pursuit of a son. That is why sex ratios are most distorted in the modern, open parts of China and India. It is also why ratios are more skewed after the first child: parents may accept a daughter first time round but will do anything to ensure their next—and probably last—child is a boy. The boy-girl ratio is above 200 for a third child in some places.

Baby girls are thus victims of a malign combination of ancient prejudice and modern preferences for small families.

How to Stop Half the Sky from Crashing Down

Baby girls are thus victims of a malign combination of ancient prejudice and modern preferences for small families. Only one country has managed to change this pattern. In the 1990s South Korea had a sex ratio almost as skewed as China's. Now, it is heading towards normality. It has achieved this not deliberately, but because the culture changed. Female education, anti-discrimination suits and equal-rights rulings made son preference seem old-fashioned and unnecessary. The forces of modernity first exacerbated prejudice—then overwhelmed it.

But this happened when South Korea was rich. If China or India—with incomes one-quarter and one-tenth Korea's levels—wait until they are as wealthy, many generations will pass. To speed up change, they need to take actions that are in their own interests anyway. Most obviously China should scrap the one-child policy. The country's leaders will resist this because they fear population growth; they also dismiss Western concerns about human rights. But the one-child limit is no longer needed to reduce fertility (if it ever was: other East Asian countries reduced the pressure on the population as much as China). And it massively distorts the country's sex ratio, with devastating results. President Hu Jintao says that creating "a harmonious society" is his guiding principle; it cannot be achieved while a policy so profoundly perverts family life.

And all countries need to raise the value of girls. They should encourage female education; abolish laws and customs that prevent daughters inheriting property; make examples of hospitals and clinics with impossible sex ratios; get women engaged in public life—using everything from television newsreaders to women traffic police. [Former Communist Chinese leader] Mao Zedong said "women hold up half the sky." The world needs to do more to prevent a gendercide that will have the sky crashing down.

9

Sex-Selective Abortion Should Be Banned

Trent Franks

Trent Franks is a Republican congressman from Arizona.

Although the practice is not nearly as widespread as it is in many Asian countries, there is evidence that certain immigrant communities in the United States are practicing sex-selective abortion so that they give birth to sons rather than daughters. The very idea of aborting a child simply because it happens to be a girl or a boy is simply appalling, and aborting a child simply because of its race, or because of the race of its parent, is equally disturbing. Such blatant gender and racial discrimination toward the unborn should be illegal in the United States. Toward that end, Congressman Trent Franks (R-Arizona) introduced House Resolution 1822, the Susan B. Anthony and Frederick Douglass Prenatal Nondiscrimination Act of 2009, which would prohibit sex-selective or race-selective abortions nationwide.

EDITOR'S NOTE: On March 30, 2011, Arizona Governor Jan Brewer signed an even stronger version of Franks' bill that makes it a felony in Arizona to perform or provide money for an abortion done for reasons of sex selection or race. Franks's HR 1822, The Susan B. Anthony and Frederick Douglass Prenatal Nondiscrimination Act of 2009, was not acted on before the end of the 111th Congressional session, so it is no longer an active bill at the national level.

Trent Franks, "A 21st-century civil-rights battle," *Washington Times*, April 20, 2009. Used by permission of Trent Franks.

The most recent U.S. census reveals that abortion clinics are engaged in an insidious form of racial and sex-based discrimination.

In a report published in the *Proceedings of the National Academy of Sciences*, Columbia University economic researchers Douglas Almond and Lena Edlund said they found a significant gender imbalance between males and females within immigrant populations in the United States, which they think provides "evidence of sex-selection, most likely at the prenatal stage."

The data revealed unnatural sex-ratio imbalances within segments of certain immigrant populations, including those originating from India, Vietnam, Thailand, Armenia and especially China, where government-enforced "one child" policies and a culturally engrained "son preference" have made sex-selection abortion so prevalent that boys outnumber girls by as much as a 2-to-1 ratio in rural communities.

What good are the hard-won liberties of voting and other women's rights if babies may still be aborted simply for being girls?

One Harvard University economist estimated that more than 100 million women were "demographically missing" from the world because of widespread and underreported practices of prenatal sex selection, an astonishing figure.

Regardless of one's position on abortion, this form of discrimination should horrify every American. The idea of killing a baby simply because she is a girl is reprehensible. Unsurprisingly, a March 2006 Zogby International poll found that 86 percent of Americans supported a prohibition on sex-selection abortion. Indeed, what good are the hard-won liberties of voting and other women's rights if babies may still be aborted simply for being girls?

Ironically, we are doing a better job internationally on this issue than we are at home. At the United Nations' 2007 annual meeting of the Commission on the Status of Women, 51st Session, the U.S. delegation spearheaded a resolution calling on countries to eliminate sex-selective abortion. The commission has urged governments of all nations "to take necessary measures to prevent . . . prenatal sex selection."

Double Standard

Congress also voiced strong disapproval of the practice when 362 members of Congress, including House Speaker Nancy Pelosi, passed a resolution in 2006 condemning the "communist government of China" for "its one-child policy, which promotes sex-selection abortion and female infanticide on a massive scale, a 'gendercide' which has led to millions of 'missing girls.'" Notwithstanding this widespread revulsion of sex-selection abortion and despite proof it occurs in America, sex-selective abortion remains legal and, therefore, tacitly condoned.

Do we realize that . . . we are contributing to the deadliest form of discrimination in our country's history . . . by systematically eliminating fully half of all blacks waiting to be born?

Abortion is being used not only to abort boys and girls just because they are boys and girls. Equally reprehensible is the reality of race-based abortion. Last spring, some federally funded clinics were exposed as agreeing to accept funds from persons who expressly asked that their donations be used to reduce the black population by abortion.

The history of the American abortion movement is replete with evidence of the purposeful placement of family planning clinics in areas with high concentrations of minorities. In fact, as many as 70 percent of abortion clinics are located in inner-city or minority neighborhoods. The impact has been devastating to black families. Fifty percent—1 in 2—of black children are aborted today in America.

A September 2008 report by the Guttmacher Institute revealed that black babies are five times likelier to be aborted than white babies. A quarter of the black population is demographically missing.

Racism in any form should cause us to recoil, but the reality of these staggering figures should make us all violently ill. Do we realize that, primarily through federally funded abortion clinics placed in our inner cities, we are contributing to the deadliest form of discrimination in our country's history against the most-discriminated-against minority in American history by systematically eliminating fully half of all blacks waiting to be born?

Congressional Action

The United States has worked hard to eliminate widespread and systematic race and sex discrimination, which we recognize as a detestable part of our past. In both race and sex discrimination, Americans ultimately responded in the strongest possible legal terms by enacting constitutional amendments to end slavery and give women the right to vote (the 14th and 19th Amendments), ending the government sanction of such discrimination. However, eliminating discriminatory practices still must be among our highest priorities.

It is past time to reject the discriminatory disgrace of aborting a child based on race or sex. To that end, I have introduced H.R. 1822, the Susan B. Anthony and Frederick Douglass Prenatal Nondiscrimination Act of 2009, which would prohibit the practice of, or solicitation or acceptance of funds for, race- or sex-selection abortion.

Americans can support the effort to address this unspoken evil by encouraging the Democratic Leadership, including

Mrs. Pelosi, and their own members of Congress to address this insidious form of discrimination by enacting this legislation.

Selecting girls and only girls for elimination or reducing the population of a given ethnic group or race distorts the entire shape of our society and undermines the entire foundation of human dignity and equality.

If we cannot find common ground on such a bedrock American principle, regardless of our differing perspectives on abortion, what hope remains?

10

Banning Sex-Selective Abortion Would Imperil Reproductive Freedom

Generations Ahead

Generations Ahead is a California-based nonprofit that works to promote the ethical use of genetic technologies by bringing together social justice advocates and organizations.

While the practice of sex-selective abortion raises some troubling issues, the best approach to limiting its use is through education and outreach, not legislative mandate. Efforts to restrict access to abortion when its purpose is sex selection are little more than a way to chip away at the reproductive rights of women in the United States, and a law prohibiting abortion because of the sex or race of the fetus would undermine a woman's right to choose. The best approach is to discourage sex selection while protecting access to abortion and reproductive choice for all women. It is important for women's movements and social justice organizations to have thoughtful dialog about the issue and to create alliances that can work together to confront this complex political challenge.

This year has brought a wave of legislation aimed at banning sex-selective abortion, sometimes in combination with bans on "race selection." The political and media circus around the racial issues and the "Black Children are an Endangered Species" billboard campaign in Georgia have been the main event lately, but it is worth understanding the specific issues around sex-selective abortion.

Generations Ahead, "Thoughts About Sex-Selective Abortion Legislation," *Collective Voices*, vol. 5, issue 11, Fall 2010. Used by permission of SisterSong.

Sex-selective abortion occurs when a pregnancy is terminated because of the sex of the fetus. While no medical test can determine the race of a fetus, the sex of a fetus may be determined by ultrasound or genetic testing such as amniocentesis. While some evidence suggests that sex selective abortions do occur in the United States, little is known about how often they occur, and whether boy or girl children are more likely to be preferred and by whom.

Efforts to ban sex-selective abortion are a threat, plain and simple.

Many reproductive health, rights, and justice advocates find the idea of sex-selective abortion troubling. From Generations Ahead's perspective, the use of sex selection to have a child of the sex the parent or parents prefer seems inexorably linked to gendered expectations about what it means to have—or be—a boy or a girl. Such practices may reinforce gender discrimination and the preference for one gender, as well as a belief that sex and gender exist only in two forms, male and female, rejecting the idea that gender is fluid.

However, we believe our best goal is to discourage the practice of sex selection while protecting access to abortion and reproductive autonomy. Efforts to ban sex-selective abortion are a threat, plain and simple. Conservative anti-abortion groups in the United States are increasingly raising the specter of sex selection as a wedge issue to attempt to divide progressive communities. At the federal level is the "Susan B. Anthony and Frederick Douglass Prenatal Nondiscrimination Act of 2009," which is Rep. Trent Franks' (R-AZ) proposed legislation to ban sex-selective and "race-selective" abortions. State legislators have also introduced similar legislation to ban such abortions in many states.

A Political Dilemma

Legislators proposing these bills have reached out to the ethnic communities most affected by sex selection and have used the language of gender equality, human rights, and preventing violence against women. State legislation presents a real political dilemma: how to oppose gender and race discrimination without aligning with explicitly anti-abortion legislators with no track record on supporting the health and well-being of women and communities of color.

When Representative Franks first introduced the Susan B. Anthony Prenatal Nondiscrimination Act, Generations Ahead, SisterSong, and National Asian Pacific American Women's Organization (NAPAWF) organized a response effort that included dozens of organizations. Many groups feared that taking a position on sex selection would undermine women's reproductive choices and identified the need for additional resources to help advocates understand the issue and be prepared for future legislative battles. When Georgia legislators introduced their own sex- and race-selective abortion legislation, accompanied by the billboard campaign, it became clear that race and sex would be closely interconnected in these fights.

While claiming to be proponents of civil rights, racial and gender equality, proponents of the legislation are relying on racist stereotypes to suggest that Black women are either so ignorant that they can be solicited to get abortions against their wills or so lacking in humanity as to be complicit in the genocide of their own people. And anti-choice advocates are activating different racist stereotypes with regards to Asian women—that they are submissive, obedient victims of their families and being coerced into abortions, or that they are so lacking in humanity to be complicit in infanticide and girl killing.

Turning the Argument Around

This issue has created an uncomfortable moment for the reproductive health, rights, and justice movements. The critical race and gender equality issues we have raised are now being raised by anti-choice advocates, who mean to use these issues against us. However, this is an opportunity for reproductive health, rights, and justice groups to work together to address health disparities, fight racism and sexism, and ensure the right and access to abortion for all women.

In the coming months, we will all be called upon to continue to wrestle with important questions about sex and gender discrimination and stereotypes, reproductive autonomy, and the ethics and wisdom of parents attempting to choose children with specific characteristics. We can't do it without building strong relationships within our own movements and with other movements—those fighting for women's rights, racial justice, human rights, and against violence against women. It is an opportunity for leadership in building new alliances and developing inclusive messages and strategies as we face this political challenge together.

Organizations to Contact

The editors have compiled the following list of organizations concerned with the issues debated in this book. The descriptions are derived from materials provided by the organizations. All have publications or information available for interested readers. The list was compiled on the date of publication of the present volume; names, addresses, phone and fax numbers, and e-mail and Internet addresses may change. Be aware that many organizations take several weeks or longer to respond to inquiries, so allow as much time as possible.

**American Congress of Obstetricians
and Gynecologists (ACOG)**
PO Box 70620, Washington, DC   20024-9998
(202) 638-5577
website: www.acog.org

The American Congress of Obstetricians and Gynecologists is the nation's leading membership group for professionals who provide health care to women. The organization advocates for quality health care for women, promotes patient education, and aims to increase awareness about women's health care. Publications include the journal *Obstetrics & Gynecology*, practice bulletins, reports, and pamphlets. ACOG's public statement on sex selection, titled "ACOG Opposes Sex Selection for Family Planning Purposes," is available on the organization's website.

American Society for Reproductive Medicine (ASRM)
1209 Montgomery Hwy., Birmingham, AL   35216-2809
(205) 978-5000 • fax: (205) 978-5005
e-mail: asrm@asrm.org
website: www.asrm.org

The American Society for Reproductive Medicine is a nonprofit organization that seeks to be a leading educator and advocate in the field of reproductive medicine. Articles about sex selection are available on its website, including "How Might We Think About Sex Selection? Case Studies and Perspectives on a Current Controversy" and "Sex Selection and Preimplantation Genetic Diagnosis." Publications include *ASRM News* and the journal *Fertility and Sterility*.

Center for Bioethics and Human Dignity

Trinity International University, 2065 Half Day Rd.
Deerfield, IL   60015
(847) 317-8180 • fax: (847) 317-8101
e-mail: info@cbhd.org
website: www.cbhd.org

The Center for Bioethics and Human Dignity is an international education center whose purpose is to offer Christian perspectives on bioethics issues. Its publications address sex selection and other reproductive technologies. The articles "Sex and Desire: The Role of Parental Aspiration in Sex Selection" and "Sex Selection Via 'Sperm-Sorting': A Morally Acceptable Option?" are available on its website.

Center for Genetics and Society

1936 University Ave., Suite 350, Berkeley, CA   94704
(510) 625-0819 • fax: (510) 665-8760
e-mail: info@geneticsandsociety.org
website: www.geneticsandsociety.org

The Center for Genetics and Society is a nonprofit organization that works to encourage genetic technologies that benefit society while opposing technologies that treat humans as commodities. It believes that sex selection can lead to social problems, such as violence against women and sex discrimination. The center works with health professionals and scientists to achieve its goals. It publishes annual reports and the newsletter *Genetic Crossroads*.

Council for Responsible Genetics (CRG)

5 Upland Rd., Suite 3, Cambridge, MA   02140
(617) 868-0870 • fax: (617) 491-5344

e-mail: crg@gene-watch.org
website: www.gene-watch.org

The Council for Responsible Genetics is a national nonprofit organization of scientists, public health advocates, and others who promote a comprehensive public interest agenda for biotechnology. Its members work to raise public awareness about issues such as genetic discrimination and patenting life forms. CRG publishes *GeneWatch* magazine and has links to articles about sex selection available on its website. Available articles include, "The Consequence of Unnatural Selection: 160 Million Missing Girls," "Are Skewed Sex Ratios in America's Future?" and "Americans Prefer Sons to Daughters, Survey Finds."

Generations Ahead

405 14th St., Suite 605, Oakland, CA   94612
(510) 832-0852
e-mail: info@generations-ahead.org
website: www.generations-ahead.org

Generations Ahead is a California-based nonprofit that works to promote the ethical use of genetic technologies by bringing together social justice advocates and organizations. The group seeks to expand the public debate and promote policies on genetic technologies that protect human rights and affirm humanity. Generations Ahead's website includes a section devoted to sex-selection issues. Resources available from the site include "Position Statement on Legislation Banning Abortion for Reasons of Sex or Race," "Position Statement on Sex Selection," and "Working Group on Race, Abortion and Sex Selection."

Genetics and Public Policy Center

1717 Massachusetts Ave. NW, Suite 530
Washington, DC   20036
(202) 663-5971 • fax: (202) 663-5992
e-mail: gppcnews@jhu.edu
website: www.dnapolicy.org

The Genetics and Public Policy Center is a nonprofit research and educational organization established in 2002 by Johns Hopkins University to help policymakers, the press, and the public understand and respond to the challenges and opportunities of genetic medicine and its potential to transform global public health. The center conducts research and policy analysis on various genetic issues, including genetic testing and new technologies in the areas of reproductive health. It has published reports on reproductive genetic testing, including *Reproductive Genetic Testing: What America Thinks* and *Reproductive Genetic Testing: Issues and Options for Policymakers*, and its website includes a bibliography with links to other studies and reports in the field, including ones dealing with sex-selection technologies and preimplementation genetic diagnosis.

The Hastings Center

21 Malcolm Gordon Rd., Garrison, NY   10524-4125
(845) 424-4040 • fax: (845) 424-4545
e-mail: mail@thehastingscenter.org
website: www.thehastingscenter.org

The Hastings Center is an independent research institute that explores the medical, ethical, and social ramifications of biomedical advances. The center publishes books, including *Reprogenetics*, the bimonthly *Hastings Center Report*, and the bimonthly newsletter *IRB: Ethics & Human Research*. Articles available on its website related to sex selection include "A Proposal for Modernizing the Regulation of Human Biotechnologies," "Assisted Reproduction," and "Enhancing Humans."

Institute for Ethics and Emerging Technologies (IEET)

Williams 119, Trinity College, 300 Summit St.
Hartford, CT   06106
(860) 297-2376
e-mail: director@ieet.org
website: www.ieet.org

The Institute for Ethics and Emerging Technologies is a Connecticut-based nonprofit that works to offset the extremism that is often present in conversations about new technologies. IEET strives to bring a rational and moderate voice to the debate about the potential benefits of new technologies while proposing realistic policies to mitigate their risks. The institute publishes the peer-reviewed *Journal of Evolution and Technology*, a monthly newsletter, several e-mail news lists, a daily blog, and a variety of podcasts. Resources available on the organization's website include the articles "Sex Selection and Women's Reproductive Rights," "Most People Favor Reproductive Technologies—But Not Sex Selection," and "[IEET Executive Director James] Hughes on Life Extension and Sex Selection."

Presidential Commission for the Study of Bioethical Issues
1425 New York Ave. NW, Suite C-100, Washington, DC   20005
(202) 233-3960 • fax: (202) 233-3990
e-mail: info@bioethics.gov
website: www.bioethics.gov

The Presidential Commission for the Study of Bioethical Issues advises the US president on bioethical matters that may emerge from advances in biomedicine and related areas of science and technology. The commission works with the goal of identifying and promoting policies and practices that ensure that scientific research, health care delivery, and technological innovation are conducted in an ethically responsible manner. The commission's website includes reports and testimony transcripts on sex selection, including "Ethical Aspects of Sex Control" and "Ethics of Emerging Diagnostic and Predictive Tools."

United Nations Population Fund (UNFPA)
605 Third Ave., New York, NY   10158
(212) 297-5000 • fax: (212) 370-0201
e-mail: hq@unfpa.org
website: www.unfpa.org

UNFPA is an international development agency that promotes policies that ensure good health, safe pregnancies and births, and respect for girls and women. Gender selection is addressed in its publications, which include the annual *State of the World Population* and other reports. Titles of interest available on the UNFPA website include "When Girls Don't Count as Much as Boys: Pre-natal Sex Selection in Viet Nam" and "Sex-Ratio Imbalance in Asia: Trends, Consequences and Policy Responses."

Bibliography

Books

Dena Davis   *Genetic Dilemmas: Reproductive Technology, Parental Choices, and Children's Futures*. New York: Oxford University Press USA, 2009.

Sarah Franklin and Celia Roberts   *Born and Made: An Ethnography of Preimplantation Genetic Diagnosis*. Princeton, NJ: Princeton University Press, 2006.

Faye Ginsburg and Rayna Rapp, eds.   *Conceiving the New World Order: The Global Politics of Reproduction*. Berkeley, CA: University of California Press, 1995.

Betsy Hartmann   *Reproductive Rights and Wrongs: The Global Politics of Population Control*, rev. ed. Boston, MA: South End, 1999.

Valerie M. Hudson and Andrea M. den Boer   *Bare Branches: The Security Implications of Asia's Surplus Male Population*. Boston, MA: MIT Press, 2004.

Mara Hvistendahl   *Unnatural Selection: Choosing Boys Over Girls, and the Consequences of a World Full of Men*. New York: PublicAffairs Press, 2011.

Marcia Inhorn and Frank van Balen, eds. — *Infertility Around the Globe: New Thinking on Childlessness, Gender, and Reproductive Technologies.* Berkeley, CA: University of California Press, 2002.

Navtej Purewal — *Son Preference: Sex Selection, Gender and Culture in South Asia.* London, United Kingdom: Berg, 2010.

Landrum Shettles and David Rorvik — *How to Choose the Sex of Your Baby.* New York: Three Rivers, 2006.

Lee Silver — *Remaking Eden: Cloning and Beyond in a Brave New World.* New York: Avon Books, 1997.

Anneke Smelik and Nina Lykke, eds. — *Bits of Life: Feminism at the Intersections of Media, Bioscience, and Technology.* New York: Routledge, 2008.

Jennifer Merrill Thompson — *Chasing the Gender Dream.* Chula Vista, CA: Aventine, 2004.

Periodicals and Internet Sources

American Society for Reproductive Medicine — "Ethics Committee Report of the American Society for Reproductive Medicine, Birmingham, Alabama," *Fertility and Sterility*, vol. 75, no. 5, May 2001.

Scott Baldauf — "India's 'Girl Deficit' Deepest Among Educated," *Christian Science Monitor*, January 13, 2006.